ESTATE PLANNING
BASICS

*A Simple, Plain English Guide
to Estate Planning Concepts*

Jeffrey G. Marsocci, Esq.

Domestic Partner Publishing, LLC

Note regarding legal counsel

As with any product, it is important to be clear about its intended purpose and use to avoid any misunderstandings. Specifically with writings about legal issues, it is noted that these materials are not a substitute for competent legal counsel. The contents of this guide are instead written to provide information about common estate planning problems faced by domestic partners, and it is designed for general educational purposes only. The contents of this guide are not to be construed as legal advice, and no attorney-client privilege exists between the reader and the author and/or publisher. In addition, laws change frequently, and therefore you also are urged to speak with an attorney about changes in the law that may affect you.

Circular 230 Disclosure: To ensure compliance with requirements imposed by the Internal Revenue Service, unless specifically indicated otherwise, any tax advice contained in this communication (including any accompanying literature) was not intended or written to be used, and cannot be used, for the purpose of avoiding tax-related penalties or promoting, marketing, or recommending to another party any tax-related matter addressed herein. For specific legal advice, you are urged to contact an attorney in your state or jurisdiction.

About the Author

Jeffrey G. Marsocci was born in Fort Worth, Texas, and raised in Lincoln, Rhode Island, where he graduated from Mount Saint Charles Academy High School. He received his Bachelor's degree in Business from Hofstra University, and two years later earned his law degree from the same university.

In 2004, he received a Certificate Degree in Non-Profit Management from Duke University, and has earned his Legal Master of Estate Preservation designation from the *Abts Institute for Estate Preservation*. Jeff also served as a member of the Legal Council for The Estate Planning Source, LLC, a nationally recognized estate preservation company formed by the protégés of the late Henry W. Abts III, trust guru and author of *The Living Trust*.

Mr. Marsocci has led his own firm in Raleigh, North Carolina, since 1996, focusing on the areas of Trusts and Estate Planning with a concentration on helping his clients plan ahead to avoid problems rather than clean them up afterwards. He also frequently participates in national and regional programs to educate attorneys, financial advisors and accountants on estate planning issues.

Jeff and his wife Kathleen work with the college-based service organization Circle K at North Carolina State University. Jeff and Kathy also each received the President's Call to Service Award for performing more than 4,000 hours of service during their lifetimes.

This guide is dedicated to Henry W. Abts III, who taught us to bring the word to all who will listen.

TABLE OF CONTENTS

Introduction

Enough is enough. People work their whole lives to accumulate assets, and when they pass on they want them to go to their loved ones. Without delays. Without red tape. Without paying huge costs. And to make this happen, smart people go to attorneys and seek the best way to give their goals life in case their life ends.

And they are being lied to.

Time and again, clients are being told by their attorneys that they don't need to bypass probate, that all they need is a Will. That their estate is too small to consider a revocable living trust to bypass the arduous, expensive and time-consuming probate process. That probate is no big deal. And time and again families are left with the death of a loved one, a visit to the attorney who drafted the Will, and then the grave-robbing begins.

But why would this happen? Aren't attorneys supposed to protect their clients? Why would attorneys betray the trust of their clients this way?

There are 25 billion and one reasons. Twenty-five billion dollars a year are lost to the probate process[1], a lot of it gobbled up greedily by probate attorneys who kept a straight face telling their clients to use Wills which turned to sly grins after death as they started filling out probate inventory forms while on the time clock.

And what about the other, the one reason? They simply don't know any better.

I don't know which is more dangerous—The attorney who knowingly does harm to his client's family by subjecting them to probate or the attorney who thinks they are doing the right thing but fail so miserably to do the research and find out the truth.

What exactly is probate?

---

[1] *The Living Trust* by Henry W. Abts III, xix, Contemporary Books, 2003.

Simply put, probate is the court process of retitling assets from a deceased person's name into the name of the proper beneficiaries. Well, that doesn't sound so terrible, does it? Well, it is. If you can think of the most circuitous and complicated route to doing something simple, probate would make it look like a quick walk around the block. Here are the downsides:

- Probate generally eats up between four and ten percent (4-10%) of the gross estate before any debts are subtracted.[2] It is also fairly typical for a law firm to charge a flat 5% to handle everything as the executor. While this does put a ceiling on the amounts a law firm will end up charging, it is a pretty high ceiling. Five percent of even a $500,000 estate would be $25,000 in fees. Most revocable living trust packages run less than $7,500 with more of them in the $5,000 range or lower.

- There are also typically delays of between 6 months and a year and a half, and often longer if the estate is governed by a Last Will and Testament that is contested.[3] Most times, the family members are waiting on receiving most probate assets for the duration of the process.

- Probate leaves plans more open to being contested. Since probate is such an elaborate bureaucracy with certain tasks that have to be completed in a set order, all it takes for someone to throw a wrench in the works is for them to file an action stating that they think something is wrong. And now the process can come to a grinding halt until their problem is taken care of. More often than we would like to think, people are paid off to go away.

---

[2] *The Living Trust* by Henry W. Abts III, page 15.

[3] *Estate Planning for Married Couples: The Legal Secrets You Need to Know to Protect Your Spouse and Your Family*, page 18

For more information, go to www.PlainEnglishAttorney.com

- Privacy is out the door when it comes to a probate estate. Because probate is a *court* process, the filings are typically open to the public. It is not uncommon for probate to require a listing of all of the deceased person's accounts, date of death values of all assets, and a listing of the names, addresses and ages of the beneficiaries. *And anyone can copy down this information.*

And there are probate attorneys who will intentionally push their clients into probate to get their piece of the $25 billion pie.

Now let me be clear about the criticisms of my own professions. There are plenty of attorneys who handle probate cases for their clients, do a good job, and work within the elaborate court bureaucracy to close out the estate. They charge a lot, but most earn every penny. Where I have the problem is when attorneys tell their clients during the planning phase that all they need are Wills knowing they'll earn large fees later on. There are plenty of attorneys who make the right recommendations but have clients who take the cheaper route of using Wills, or, worse still, just don't put a plan in place at all.

As far as I'm concerned, their families are paying the price for their loved one's lack of planning. They are still victims of the probate system, but only because someone else ignored all of the books, advice, news articles and television shows telling them to put a plan in place, and now because of their failure to act they have to deal with the fallout. Yes, the family members are victims, but more like the family members of deceased person died during a flood because they refused a police order to evacuate their home as opposed to the family members of an airplane crash victim. Both are terrible situations, but there is an element of choice on the part of the person dying in the flood.

No, where there is a true need for rebellion is against the attorneys who know better and try to hide their smiles while recommending Wills.

"Your estate is less than $5 million, so you don't need a trust…"[4] That's like saying you don't need to change the oil in your car because the gas tank is full. The $5 million has to do with estate taxes and a revocable living trust is about avoiding probate. *What's the attorney thinking? Large legal fees!*

"Don't worry about it. Probate fees in our state are not that high…"[5] What they're saying is the fees that a court charges is not that high compared to other states. But they are pocketing most of the $25 billion a year, not the court itself charging filing fees. *What's the attorney thinking? HUGE legal fees!*

Or

"A trust is too complicated for your situation…"[6] What they are actually saying is that they are not skilled or learned enough to produce or interpret a good revocable living trust. *Plus they are thinking, TREMENDOUS legal fees!*

Enough is enough. It is time for the public to push back against this $25 billion a year industry being surreptitiously slipped onto people who want to plan ahead, who want to make things easier for their family, and are instead being lied to by legal professionals more interested in filling their own coffers at the expense of depleting yours. It is time for us to proclaim loudly that probate is not necessary, we will plan to avoid it, and we're no longer going to listen to lies and falsehoods against our family's interests. It is time for a rebellion against the dishonest elements of our legal profession.

If you want to join this revolution, then please keep reading and take action. Your family does not have to be part of the $25 billion boondoggle pressed on the public each year. But the decisions is entirely up to you.

---

[4] Just about every attorney who earned more than $10,000 on a probate case.

[5] Attorneys from all 50 states.

[6] Condescending attorneys from all 50 states.

For more information, go to www.PlainEnglishAttorney.com

Chapter One:
The Probate Court Process

The children sat around the conference table, extremely upset at what they were being told. Months of court proceedings ahead, thousands upon thousands of dollars in legal fees, and all of his private financial information exposed to the public. Three middle-aged heirs of their father's estate were looking around for someone to blame, and it was becoming increasingly clear their father and real estate attorney were at fault.

"Your father met with us, and we outlined a plan to do things the right way," the attorney calmly said. "You obviously found the papers from the seminar we held, and that is how we met your father. I recommended a revocable living trust to handle his estate wishes, stressed the proper titling of accounts and beneficiary designations, and your father even attended a specific seminar on the complexities of the probate process."

"Here is the letter he wrote me declining my services," the attorney said, passing the hand-written letter across the table to the oldest son. "He decided to go with a Last Will and Testament through the attorney that handled his house closing. Apparently, his attorney told him probate was no big deal and that he, the other attorney, could do a plan that addressed all of your father's issues for a few hundred dollars."

"I don't understand this," the daughter said, the frustration of the whole situation getting to her. "My father was told by his attorney that he didn't need a trust and that probate was not expensive nor was it a big deal. Then we go to him after our father dies and he asks for $20,000 just to start!"

She took a breath, the attorney nodding his head in understanding. "Everything but the IRA is going through probate, two attorneys are telling us it will take about a year, and it's probably going to cost about $70,000 to administer this thing, and my father, who was a very private person, is going to have all of his finances open to the world," the daughter said. "Why? Wasn't a Will supposed to take care of this?"

"Your father fell into one of the biggest traps out there," the attorney said. "By listening to an attorney who had his own best interests at heart in collecting legal fees later, your father paid less to have a Will and now his estate is paying the price. I'm sorry, but that's the way it is."

The younger brother got up from the table and walked out, too frustrated to stay quiet and unwilling to hear any more.

The older brother sat back into the chair, tapping his pen on the table for a moment, holding back tears and trying to ask the next questions. "If he had done the planning you suggested, would he have avoided the court process?"

"Yes," the attorney said without hesitation.

"How... how much would the planning have cost?" the brother asked next, his sister starting to cry into her hands.

"A little less than $5,000," the attorney said

"How much would it have cost to settle the trust?"

"Maybe a few hundred dollars."

Probate is evil. Fire, brimstone, from the pits of hell, evil.

At least that's how many people feel when a loved one's estate is going through the process. Especially when they start writing checks to attorneys for legal fees… or each time the date of death hits a six month anniversary and the estate is still not settled… or they get yet another round of papers to sign. In all, people see the process as expensive, time-consuming, intrusive, frustrating, and completely worthless.

As an attorney, I can not agree more, and I wish more of my fellow attorneys felt the same way. Unfortunately, many of my colleagues either do not handle much estate planning and so stick to writing Wills, guaranteeing probate for their clients; or worse, they understand what will happen to their clients and they are hoping for large legal fees to handle the paperwork for the probate estate. I discussed the downsides of probate in the Introduction, so there is no need to repeat it here, but…

In the end for the family, probate is still evil.

But the probate process did not start out with that in mind. What it did was provide a framework to make sure that people did not steal from the estate and that the correct beneficiaries received their inheritance. Simple enough. But what it devolved into was a huge labyrinth of paperwork wrapped in an enigma and sealed over with bureaucracy, and it now takes the "expert" in the form of an attorney to decipher the probate code and give the court pieces of paper before it gives up money to the rightful beneficiaries. But, again, what exactly is probate?

In short, probate is the legal court process governed by a State that oversees the transfer of title from a deceased person the appropriate beneficiary or beneficiaries. Despite the inventories, despite the appraisals, and despite the huge administrative expenses, it is nothing more than an elaborate retitling process. A gigantic, burdensome, pain in the behind, retitling process.

Probate Procedures

The probate court process varies widely and greatly from state to state, so there is no single correct answer to the procedures of probate. However, many of the different states have a few similar characteristics in their procedures. Whatever you do, do not take what is written here as fact for your state or jurisdiction. While there are other components of this guide that are fairly universal across 50 states, such as the concepts of revocable living trusts and powers of attorney, you should find books or talk to an attorney about the process in your particular state.

With that said, some of the similarities are:

1) Qualification of the Personal Representative

2) Inventory of Assets on Date of Death

3) Notification of Creditors and Beneficiaries

4) Accounting of Assets Received and Debts Paid

5) Disbursement of Assets to the Beneficiaries

Qualification of the Personal Representative

The executor, administrator, personal representative, or whatever else the position held by a person may be called, it all is the same in that a court has to put its official stamp of approval on the person for them to get anything done. The term "executor" (or executrix) usually applies to a person executing the terms of a Last Will and Testament. The term "administrator" usually applies to the person handling an estate where the person didn't even have a Will. The term "personal representative" applies to either instance and is quickly becoming the industry standard term for the person in charge of any kind of estate.

During this initial phase of the probate process, people are named or volunteer to handle the administration of the estate and the court imposes its procedures in choosing the right person for the job. Typically, the court has little in the form of criteria relevant to the job and relies more on how closely the person applying is related to the deceased person to screen them in and then looks at criteria such as felonies or other crimes to screen people out. Regardless, the court has to choose someone, and there is relevant information required to make that determination.

[With a revocable living trust, as long as the person named as successor trustee is not dead, incompetent, or in jail, they take over. No forms, procedures or inventories required to start managing assets.]

Inventory of Assets on Date of Death

Regardless of the state or jurisdiction, the probate court wants to know, at a minimum, about the assets subject to probate. All of those assets still titled in the deceased person's name after their death must be included in inventories.

In some states or jurisdictions, the court wishes to also know about other assets that bypass the probate system, such as accounts titled as joint property or which have a beneficiary designation on them if for no other reason than to have the information on hand in case the estate is sued. If all of the assets in probate are not sufficient enough to pay debts, then most states allow non-probate assets to be attached to pay those debts.

In my home state of North Carolina, all joint property assets and accounts must be listed on an initial inventory when a person is filing to become the personal representative.[7] Down the road, the court also wants to see the "signature cards" for joint accounts to "prove" that they bypassed the probate system. That's right. If you are using joint property to bypass the probate court system, the probate court system wants you to file an equivalent amount of paperwork to prove you bypassed the system.

The biggest exception to this rule in North Carolina is a revocable living trust. Since the technical "owner" on the account is the trust and not the deceased person, then it is not subject to probate disclosure in the inventories.

Notification of Creditors and Beneficiaries

In some fashion or another, all creditors and beneficiaries of the deceased person's estate must be notified of the person's death and told that they may be a creditor or beneficiary of the estate. The process varies from state to state, but most states require a direct notification of the beneficiaries and some posting of a notice to creditors in a newspaper that the person has died.

---

[7] Form AOC-E-201. http://www.nccourts.org/Forms/Documents/376.pdf

This second form of notification often becomes handy for estates since there is only a limited time for the creditors to file claims before they are cut off. But it does cost money, particularly if the person had a lot of creditors. By far the easier and less costly procedure is to pay off all legitimate debts and move on. If there are any debts that are not legitimate, let the person trying to get something for nothing file a claim against the trust and fight it out there. Typically people who are trying to scam an estate are too lazy to participate in a court action and will refuse to put up their own money to file one in the first place.

Accounting of Assets Received and Debts Paid

So far, the work described for probate has been extensive, but now the red tape will start to strangle all who unwittingly wade into probate thinking it is no big deal. The probate court requires that all money received by the estate is accounted for, that all money spent by the estate is accounted for, and, typically, receipts and cancelled checks have to be submitted to the court for approval. Every single one.

In addition to all of the receipts and cancelled checks being submitted for every expense from the floral arrangements for the funeral down to paying the accountant for preparing income taxes, all of these items have to be compiled into an inventory. It's sort of like a person giving all of their receipts and cancelled checks to an IRS agent... that's fine, but they want the tax return filled out with all of the items listed. Every single one.

In the end, when the inventories are being filed to account for all of the money received and disbursed, the court wants to have these transactions clearly noted with balances. Everything has to balance out financially, and every penny must be accounted for. Every single one. (Believe me, it is not as easy as it sounds.)

Disbursement of Assets to the Beneficiaries

In the end, there is a phase where all of the remaining assets are turned over to the beneficiaries. This is typically done at the end of the process, but many states allow some of the assets to be distributed well ahead of closing the estate, but again everything must be balanced, fair, and provide receipts with it.

Many courts insist on their own forms being used to document a beneficiary receiving their inheritance, and sometimes those forms have to be notarized. While not a big deal by itself, one uncooperative beneficiary can hold up the closing of the probate estate. The process itself is complicated enough for the average person to comprehend. But what makes it most complicated is when these individual transactions hold up the entire process.

I once helped a daughter probate her mother's estate, and the funeral home was not being cooperative. The probate court insisted that a receipt from the funeral home show a zero balance at the bottom of a billing statement. We kept telling the funeral home exactly what we needed, and instead of showing a billing statement with a zero balance they kept showing the final bill with several thousands of dollars owed and a stamp marked "paid in full." Three times we had to request exactly what we needed, putting the request in writing each time and showing a sample bill, and still they sent the same exact statement. The probate estate was held up four months, and we had to charge at least another $1,000 for our efforts because of the uncooperative funeral home. And that kept us from paying out the final amounts to the family.

Summary

The probate process varies greatly from state to state, and complications always seem to pop up. No matter what an individual probate attorney says about the system in their state being different, don't be fooled. I don't have to say that probate is evil. The people who have taken a loved one's estate through the process will tell you so.

Chapter Two:
Myths of Probate

Charles and Barbara were together for 20 years, and they prided themselves on taking care of all of the little details. Charles was a successful architect, Barbara kept their home and their small arts and crafts business going, and both of them made sure all of their records were complete and accurate to a fault. They even had a commitment ceremony three years into their relationship but chose not to legally marry. But a few years ago, they took additional steps based on advice they received from some friends. They placed Charles's house into joint property with a right of survivorship with Barbara, drafted Wills through the attorney who handled a speeding ticket for Charles, and set up a system of depositing money into Barbara's account to handle the household expenses. After talking with their friends and seeing what they did, they were sure they were covered.

Now, 3 years later, Barbara is sitting in the lawyer's office crying. It has been 8 months since Charles died and she is still unable to get to any of the accounts because they are all going through the probate court system. The house was all Barbara's, but the mortgage payments were a few months in arrears and there was a threat of foreclosure. The other bills were falling behind, and now her part-time business that was more of a hobby is now a full time necessity to put food on the table. Further, Charles's brother is contesting the Will the attorney recommended, dragging out the proceedings and making life difficult for Barbara.

"What did we do wrong?" Barbara asked her attorney.

A large part of my legal practice involves helping people plan their lives and estates to avoid complicated, costly, and frustrating bureaucracies whenever possible. The crème de la crème of bureaucracies is probate, a nightmare for any family. When someone passes on with assets titled in their name, their assets have to go through the probate court inventory process before going to the eventual heirs. *This happens regardless if a person has a Last Will and Testament or not.* In fact, a Last Will and Testament is nothing more than a person ordering a court to take their assets through that bureaucracy.

In general, probate is costly, time-consuming, and causes a loss of privacy. National studies vary greatly, but I am comfortable estimating the average cost of probate as totaling between 4% and 10% of assets.[8] While married couples typically have some relief when one spouse dies in that there are often few assets subject to probate, the costs kick in when the second spouse dies and assets go to the next generation. For unmarried couples, these assets are often subject to the same level of expenses twice.

Probate is also time-consuming, often taking between six and eighteen months before finally being completed. For family members, this may be an interminable wait, especially if the beneficiaries were financially dependant on the deceased person. In addition to being costly and time-consuming, probate also discloses much more information than most people are comfortable with. Every bank account, parcel of real estate, mutual fund and other assets in probate must list the financial institution, the account number, and the date of death balance. All beneficiaries must have their name, address, and age listed on the court forms as well. And because these are court documents, they are open to the public. Most people do not wish to have this information out there for the world to see, but that is what probate requires.

But there is hope in avoiding the probate process altogether by using a Revocable Living Trust instead of a Last Will and Testament. By using and taking control of a Revocable Living Trust and having title to assets in the name of the trust, these assets can avoid probate and all of the negatives that go along with it.

---

[8] *The Living Trust* by Henry W. Abts III, page 15.

Over the last seventeen years of practicing law, I have heard of many attorneys disparaging revocable living trusts using a variety of pretexts. The four biggest are listed here, but before going into them I would like to make two points. First, why would attorneys recommend a Will if it means a complicated, costly and time consuming process? The most likely answer is that attorneys can make lots of money navigating this process for their clients, and legal fees typically comprise most of the 4% to 10% mentioned before. Why just take $5,000 for a revocable living trust package now when they can get $20,000 to $50,000 on a half million dollar probate estate later? The other possibility is they simply do not realize just how negatively probate impacts their clients and their families.

Second, I want to point out that I have no problem with attorneys who take on the rough task of handling probate for their clients. They typically earn every penny that they charge. What I have a problem with are attorneys who, *in the planning phase*, tell their clients that probate is no big deal, something I know to be false. These people are setting up their clients to have their grave robbed… by them and the state. The probate attorneys who know how horrible probate is and yet recommend Wills to their clients are evil. They are putting their own financial interest ahead of yours and your family's, and they amount to nothing more than grave robbers.

And now, the four biggest myths told by probate attorneys:

Probate Myths

Probate Myth 1. *"Probate fees are not that high in our state"*

While technically true, this statement is highly deceptive. In North Carolina, probate fees are 40 cents for each $100 of personal property and accounts with a maximum fee of $6,000. However, these are the direct fees imposed by the probate court and have nothing to do with the fees attorneys charge for their work, and this is how it is in most states. The next time an attorney suggests a Last Will and Testament rather than a Revocable Living Trust because "probate fees are not that high," have the attorney put in writing an all-inclusive price quote for their firm to handle probate for the estate. And then watch as their expression changes and the disclaimers start.

Probate Myth 2. "If you have less than $5 million, then you don't need a revocable living trust."

This is like telling someone that they don't need to change the oil in their car because the gas tank is full. The $5 million limit probate attorneys reference has to do with estate taxes and has nothing to do with avoiding the problems associated with probate. (Attorneys may also quote a lower number, and that typically has to do with the estate tax limits for their state whereas the $5 million or so is the federal estate tax). The statement becomes nothing more than a smoke screen to avoid the fundamental question the attorney is being asked, namely can a revocable living trust be used to make things easier and less costly for the family.

While trusts can assist with avoiding unnecessary estate taxes, the primary purpose of a revocable living trust is to avoid probate. Twice for a couple using a joint trust. If an attorney is referencing the federal estate tax exemptions when asked whether or not you need a revocable living trust, they are 1) intentionally misleading you, or 2) they are so weak in knowledge and experience in life and estate planning matters that they really believe you don't need a trust based solely on the level of assets, or 3) they care so little about doing a good job that they'll parrot what they've been told by other attorneys without giving any thought to the advice they are giving. I'm not sure which of the three is the worst.

Probate Myth 3. "A trust is too complicated for your situation."

While a Revocable Living Trust is more complicated to set up than a Will, the complicated part is for the attorney to set it up properly and explain it. It is only in rare instances when people have next to no financial assets that a revocable living trust may be too complicated for their particular situation. One or two low-valued accounts can likely be handled with beneficiary designations or joint property without issue, but if you are reading this guide then that is probably not your situation.

Do not take the "too complicated" statement with blind faith from an attorney. Be sure to go into detail why they feel your situation is too complicated, and you will likely find that the only complication is they are not equipped to construct a proper revocable living trust for you and explain it. Of course, if you want to see complicated, take a look at a probate file sometime.

Probate Myth 4. "If you want to avoid probate, just use joint property."

While joint property with a right of survivorship avoids probate upon the first death, both of these techniques use what I call "one-step planning." It is only good once, and none of the other eventualities and contingencies that you may want can be put into effect.

Since joint property with a right of survivorship only works to transfer the property to the survivor once, what happens if both people pass on together? Probate happens. What if one person only wants the assets to be available for the survivor for their lifetime and then the remainder goes to other people? Joint property can not do this. What if you want the property to go to a beneficiary who is younger but want it supervised until they reach a certain age? Joint property can not do this. What if you want property to go equally to your children, which is common, and one of the children passes on before you? Most people want the deceased child's children, their grandchildren, to receive the property, but this would leave them cut out.

The joint property piecemeal approach guarantees multiple instances of potentially costly planning to get exactly what you want whereas a revocable living trust can both avoid probate and lay out multiple situations, scenarios, and levels of beneficiaries.

In addition to joint property having all of the drawbacks of one step planning, it can also come with costly gift taxes for non-spouses. When one person "puts their child's name on" the deed to their house, they are actually giving a gift of half of the value of the house. This gift comes with gift taxes if the value of the gifts from one partner to the other exceeds $14,000 in any given year. Retitling a $500,000 paid up house from one parent to the parent and child with a right of survivorship is a gift of $250,000, only $14,000 of which is exempt. Depending on state taxes, the tax on this one item is far in excess of what it costs to complete an entire revocable living trust estate plan for both parents to avoid probate for nearly all of their assets, plan out all of the contingencies they desire, and do so without incurring gift taxes.

The legal odds are already stacked against people with the probate court system. Using a Last Will and Testament or other piecemeal approaches to planning rather than using a comprehensive Revocable Living Trust only imposes more costs, delays, and public disclosure of personal information than is necessary. So next time you hear one of these myths of probate, be sure to get the attorney to assure *in writing* that:

- probate for two estates will cost less than a joint revocable living trust,

- that there will be no time delays, and

- that all of your financial information will remain private.

In the years of telling people to get those assurances from probate attorneys, I have yet to see one guarantee.

Living Trust Myths

In the interest of fair play, there are also a lot of myths about revocable living trusts out there. While a revocable living trust can tremendously help families save on legal fees, taxes, and other expenses, it is not a magical, legal entity.

While it is fortunate that the public is becoming more aware of alternatives to the Last Will and Testament to avoid probate, there is a large revocable trust industry developed by life insurance companies, and life insurance salespeople are using seminars on revocable living trusts simply to sell expensive life insurance policies and annuities. It is extremely unfortunate that a lot of these presentations are not given by (or even reviewed by) estate planning attorneys who have the best interests of the clients at heart, and with the primary goal being making a sale the salesperson may lie or provide a guarantee that is simply not true. This may even be worse than the probate attorneys because these salespeople are using a good concept to make a sale on something else, and they'll lie to do it.

It is here that half-truths and patently false statements about trusts are made, and while properly drafted and executed revocable living trusts can do much, these documents are not omnipotent fortresses of life and estate planning designed to protect people from every evil that may befall them. Here are the biggest three myths about revocable living trusts.

Trust Myth 1: _"A Revocable Living Trust Avoids All Estate Taxes"_. While it would be nice to have a single trust where someone could simply put all of their assets into it, keep complete control of the trust, and it would be completely exempt from any estate taxes at all, ever. However, such a trust simply does not exist. This misconception probably stems from the mistaken belief that avoiding probate means avoiding taxes, and therefore if you avoid one you must automatically be avoiding the other. Not true.

The distinction between avoiding probate and avoiding taxes is most easily seen when looking at "title" to assets versus "control" of assets. If a person passes on and something is titled in an individual's name, then it must go through the probate court process before getting to the end beneficiaries. In order for the title, or "ownership papers," to go from the deceased person to their beneficiaries, the probate court has to officially transfer title. If the deceased person had all of their assets titled in the name of their revocable living trust, then there is no "title" for the probate court to pass along... everything is handled outside of court through the terms and conditions of the trust.

As complicated, time-consuming, and frustrating the probate court process can be, it has nothing to do with another of life's great tragedies—taxes. Estate taxation is based on "control" over an asset rather than "title." If a person has control over an asset when they pass on, then it is counted as part of their taxable estate, *regardless of how actual title is held and whether or not it went through probate.* Therefore, if a person holds title to their house, checking account and mutual fund in the name of their revocable living trust and they maintain complete control over the trust, then their house, checking account and mutual fund will avoid the probate process when it is transferred to their partner. However, the value of their house, checking account and mutual fund will be counted as part of their taxable estate.

There are some potential death tax breaks married couples and partners can take advantage of in the revocable living trusts, but this is a subject for another time. For more information, read about credit shelter trusts for married couples in *Estate Planning for Married Couples* and SECURE trusts for unmarried domestic partners in *Estate Planning for Domestic Partners,* both at www.PlainEnglishAttorney.com and at online bookstores.

Trust Myth 2: *Assets in a Revocable Living Trust are exempt from lawsuits*. While this would be fantastic, particularly for those who are business owners, a revocable living trust does *not* exempt assets from lawsuits. Again, this comes down to title versus control, and since people setting up their revocable living trust maintain complete control over their trust assets, those assets are not exempt from being taken in a lawsuit.

This misconception probably comes from intentionally or unintentionally vague seminars. The kernel of truth about assets being exempt from lawsuits refers not to the people who create the trust and run it as trustees, but instead applies to the beneficiaries who would receive the trust assets when the second spouse or partner passes on. Well-drafted trusts will protect assets from being distributed to beneficiaries involved in lawsuits or a bankruptcy.

While people may not be able to use a revocable living trust to protect their personal assets from business lawsuits, there is actually a simpler, more common solution which is to incorporate the business. By establishing a corporation or limited liability company and keeping business operations and funds separate from personal matters, people can protect their personal assets from most business lawsuits.

Trust Myth 3: *Assets in a revocable living trust are protected from Medicaid spend down rules*. While the first two myths are probably derived from confusing issues of title and control, this myth is probably perpetuated more by confusing the revocable living trust with other trusts specifically designed to shelter assets if someone needs to go to a nursing home and wishes for Medicaid to pay for the expenses. (Without going too much into the complexities of the Medicaid program, let me give the short and incomplete summary that Medicaid will handle nursing home bills provided you have little or no assets of value.) The revocable living trust helps people with the management and distribution of assets if one or both become incapacitated or pass on. A catastrophic illness trust can preserve assets for the benefit of a person in case they become ill and need the long-term care contemplated by the federal Medicaid program.

The differences between these two kinds of trusts are stark. With a revocable living trust, people can maintain complete control over their trust assets throughout their lifetimes. With a catastrophic illness trust, a person would have to give up complete control when the assets go into the trust. With a revocable living trust, the people can amend or revoke the trust at any time. With a catastrophic illness trust, the trust is permanent and unchangeable once established. With a revocable living trust, the people can be the trustees of the trust. With a catastrophic illness trust, someone else must be the trustee. Finally, for the catastrophic illness trust to even work, the assets going into the trust must be transferred five years before Medicaid is even applied for.

"I don't like that," is what I usually hear from clients when I describe the terms of a catastrophic illness trust. The fact is the rules for a person to qualify for Medicaid care have become so strict in making sure a person has very little in assets that it is almost not worth trying. Almost. There are some potential solutions for Medicaid qualification depending on your specific situation, but they do not usually fit into a simple solution. But the solution is definitely not a revocable living trust by itself.

There are some extremely important benefits available in life and estate planning with the right kind of revocable living trust, but it is not a solution to *all* potential problems. A revocable living trust fits many more situations than most probate attorneys will let on, but all of the myths should be known.

Probate Avoidance Myths

Finally, there are also myths surrounding different ways to avoid probate that are not so effective. Sometimes conventional wisdom is not so wise, and it takes more than advice from a friend to handle things the right way. Unfortunately, a lot of layperson advice on avoiding probate gets followed because it sounds simple and, in the area of life and estate planning, the problems are not realized until years later, often when it is too late to do anything about it.

Probate Avoidance Myth 1: Using Joint Property

If you own a home and want someone to inherit the home without probate, the urge may be to "put them on the deed" to the house with a right of survivorship. The same holds for bank and financial accounts, and changing the ownership to "joint with a right of survivorship" can also avoid probate. And it can be done without an attorney. Wow! Simple? Yes. Effective? *No.*

What joint property fails to account for is the federal gift tax that allows only the first $14,000 (in the year this guide was published) given from one person to a non-spouse without the tax being imposed. Every dollar after that is subject to a gift tax. However, the federal government, in all of its renowned mercy, graciously allows $5 million to be gifted over the course of your life without you actually having to pay the tax. The downside is it also lowers the amount dollar-for-dollar you are allowed to pass on without estate taxes upon death.

Before you tune out completely because of the five million dollar exemption, the real danger here is not the actual payment of tax, but the failure to file a gift tax form with the IRS. Because of two of the IRS's favorite words "interest" and "penalties," it is best to stay above board on all of these transactions. The other reason for reading on and keeping gifts to less than $14,000 a year is to avoid having to recreate records when the IRS audits a person's estate and finds multiple gifts without a gift tax form being filled out. If you record all transactions properly and avoid situations where gifts of $14,000 or more per year are made between partners, then you can prevent huge accounting bills in the event of IRS action.

Please note this is only related to federal gift taxes. There may be state-level gift taxes as well. For more information on how the gift tax may affect you in your own state, please see a qualified accountant or CPA in your area for specific tax advice.

Another drawback to joint property with a right of survivorship is it only looks one step ahead. When one person passes on, the other will receive the property, but what happens if both people pass on together? The property will have to go through probate before it can be distributed to the intended beneficiaries. Good life and estate planning looks more than one step ahead to cover multiple contingencies and avoid probate for all of them, and good life and estate planning attorneys will look more than one step ahead. With the right revocable living trust, the property can be titled in the name of the trust, all of these contingencies can be spelled out, and the property will go where it was intended without probate.

Probate Avoidance Myth 2: Beneficiary Designations

In an effort to make things simple and avoid probate on accounts and life insurance, many institutions allow their clients to name beneficiaries on the accounts, and many even allow a place to indicate a contingent beneficiary. While this is good for the client, it is also good for the company because now it is not in the middle of a probate proceeding that may be contested. Legally, the company is fulfilling its obligation after the death of the client once it transfers the account to the new named owner. In most cases, and depending on the company, it is a quick process taking a few days to handle the paperwork and make the transfer.

While beneficiary designations are not as lethal to some plans as Wills and joint property with a right of survivorship, there are still some drawbacks to using beneficiary designations rather than a revocable living trust. As mentioned before with joint property, it only accounts for one transfer upon the death of the owner. If and when the owner passes on, it will go to the person or persons listed as the beneficiary. What if that person passes on before them? Financial institutions which allow for contingent beneficiaries have let the client take care of the first "what if" by listing a contingent beneficiary, but what if this beneficiary passes on as well?

By using a revocable living trust, *all* of the different contingencies can be listed within the trust, and now the account is handled properly, without probate, regardless of how many years pass by and how many different people may have passed on. Depending on the type of account, the account can either be placed into the trust directly or the beneficiary designation features on the account can name the trust as the beneficiary upon death. Now the account can stay in the individual person's name during life and name the trust as beneficiary upon death. The different methods of funding a revocable living trust include changing beneficiary designations the right way.

There is another serious drawback to using beneficiary designations. Most parents understand that while they love their children and they may be legal adults at 18, most 18 year olds are not responsible enough to effectively handle a large inheritance. By placing a child's name on a beneficiary designation, the child gets control of the account at age 18 should anything happen to the parent. If instead a revocable living trust was listed as the beneficiary, a trustee would manage this account for until the beneficiary reaches a more suitable age, such as 30 or 35 years of age.

Summary

We have now covered the four biggest probate myths, the three most prominent misconceptions about revocable living trusts, and two probate avoidance techniques that are defective at best. In this case, knowledge is power in the anti-probate revolution, and by dispensing with the myths, misconceptions and outright lies, we can focus on the truth. Next we will review the revocable living trust in detail to see how things can be done the right way.

Chapter Three:
The Revocable Living Trust

Two years ago, I was reviewing a lease agreement for a client's new restaurant and my receptionist buzzed through, asking if I had a minute to talk with someone on the phone about his mother-in-law's estate. She mentioned that he was referred by another attorney we knew who handled real estate closings, so I told her I would take the call.

His frustration was immediate. As he spoke, it was clear he didn't even want to make the call, but his wife was making him. The main thing was his wife was sure her mother had a life insurance policy, and 'a long time ago' she was told by her mother that she was the beneficiary. "I can't find out anything about her estate, and it's just not right what's going on."

I asked a few more questions about where he checked for information. They called the clerk of courts office and was told that the executor had been appointed but there was no other information on the assets. They checked a few insurance companies the wife remembered seeing bills for a long time ago to see if there was a policy, and they were told they could not give out that information to anyone but the executor.

"Well, something doesn't sound quite right," I told him. "Who is the executor?"

He paused for a minute, as if trying to figure out whether or not to tell me something, and he said, "That woman who calls herself her partner is the executor, and I tell you it just ain't right that her daughter can't get information."

As he explained how it shouldn't matter that they barely spoke in the last five years and that no matter what that woman called herself, she was not family, and how could everything be distributed within a few weeks, I was starting to see where this was going. Nonetheless, I wanted to make sure of the legal situation, even though I had already decided not to take the case. I asked, "If her estate is going through probate, then the asset list is publicly available. Are you sure her estate is in probate, meaning she used a Will to handle distributing her assets?"

I heard some papers shuffling in the background. "The lady at the court told me that her property was in some kind of... wait a minute and let me look... yeah, a revocable living trust. What the hell is that?"

I then went on to explain that a revocable living trust avoids the probate court system, is private, and if it were anything like the trusts we draft and his mother-in-law's partner was the trustee, then there was probably very little he could do. He then politely thanked me for my time and hung up while mumbling "it just ain't right."

The Revocable Living Trust is quickly growing in popularity among most middle class families of all kinds wishing to save their heirs time, taxes, and probate costs. But, despite efforts to keep the existence of these trusts quiet by many in the legal profession, the revocable living trust is nothing new. The first recorded instances of trusts was circa 800 A.D. in the Roman Empire, and then adopted in the 12th Century in England to prevent the arbitrary confiscation of land by the crown. And speaking of revolutionary, the first recorded instance of a trust being used in the New World was created by a local attorney in Hanover County, Virginia in 1765. You may have heard of the attorney. His name was Patrick Henry. By no means is the revocable living trust a new entity.

These versatile trusts are today created during life and upon death distribute property much the same way probate does through a Will, but it does so without probate court supervision or interference, and, most importantly for some, keeping the hands of probate attorneys out of their family's pockets. Instead, a less expensive, less time consuming process of settling a revocable living trust is used, and your successor trustee signs title to the assets over to the heirs.

For more information, go to www.PlainEnglishAttorney.com

Taking an estate through probate can be a time-consuming, expensive and frustrating process. It seems that the only people that come out ahead by taking an estate through probate is the law firm handling the paperwork. However, a probate court only takes control of and examines property titled in the deceased person's name. If everything is titled in the name of a revocable living trust rather than the deceased person's name, then the court does not have to be involved (as long as the bills are paid and no one contests the estate plan). The Living Trust document then tells people how the estate should be distributed, outside of court, and with as little fuss as possible. If you have the right attorney to set things up correctly in the first place.

Finding the right attorney

Many attorneys are somewhat familiar with revocable living trusts as a concept, but there are far fewer attorneys who know the true advantages of a trust. Worse still, there are some attorneys who know these advantages, but they would prefer to keep their clients with Wills in order to get the lucrative probate legal work later. I previously mentioned that approximately 4-10% of most estates are eaten up by the probate process. The lion's share of those costs is in attorney fees. While there are many more attorneys who do not fully understand the benefits of a revocable living trust and are giving them the best advice they have regarding estate planning, there are some attorneys who are making recommendations in their own financial best interest when they tell clients they do not need a trust.

Also, unlike other areas of law, it is difficult for an attorney to know if he or she did something wrong until it is too late to do anything about it. If a real estate transaction is messed up, there is a good chance someone will catch it before the closing. If an attorney messes up on procedure in a divorce, it is likely an opposing attorney, a clerk or the judge will point out this mistake. Unless another attorney proficient in life and estate planning reviews your documents, there is usually no one else in the process who would know what was wrong until the documents were needed. And once a person is deceased or incapacitated, there is little, if anything, that can be done.

It is always a good idea to sit down with an attorney and ask questions before hiring one. In order to help you find the right attorney and other professionals in putting together your life and estate plan, you and your spouse should look for the following warning signs:

- They recommend using joint property with a right of survivorship or beneficiary designations.

- They tell you all you need are wills and you shouldn't even discuss a trust.

- They say probate is not a big deal and their firm handles probate cases all of the time.

If you notice any of these points, they clearly don't have the knowledge to help with life and estate planning. This is not to say they are bad lawyers, but I've seen lawyers who are very good with real estate matters, or family law, or traffic court cases want to help when their clients come to them with another matter like drafting life and estate planning documents. The problem is they don't realize it is not that simple.

The summer after I turned 16, I went to work in a pizza place. Before I started working, I thought it couldn't be so difficult to make a pizza. What's involved, after all? You put it in the oven for a certain amount of time at a certain temperature, and then take it out, cut and serve. No big deal, right? Wrong.

Then I saw the process up close. You go from taking a ball of pizza dough kept at a certain temperature, to using just the right amount and mix of flour, to stretching the dough using just the right amount of pressure and movements, to placing the dough on a flat wooden board with a handle, to having just the right amount of raised dough at the edge to form a good crust, to putting just the right amount of sauce and cheese on the dough, to placing the board into the oven and giving it the right shaking movement to be able to pull the board out from under the pizza without stretching it into an oval, to cooking it just the right amount of time at 500 degrees, and then taking it out properly with a metal plate on a wooden handle, placing it on a metal plate for serving, and then cutting it properly.

Procedures may have changed some since I was 16, and some pizza places handle some of the process before the pizza ingredients make it to the restaurant. But back then, it took a lot of time and practice for me to learn this process and handle it properly. To this day, I still remember it takes six minutes for a large cheese pizza to cook, eight and a half minutes for a pizza with "the works" to cook, and the dough should be as close as possible to 62 degrees. The point is, I never would have realized it took so much to make a pizza unless I was shown how to do it, and I wouldn't have realized how little I did know until a horrible looking (and horribly tasting) pizza came out of the oven the first time. It is the same with attorneys practicing in an area not thoroughly studied. It may look easy on the surface, but until they see the first life and estate plan in action, they won't know what kind of job they did.

While there are a lot of lawyers not able to truly handle advanced life and estate planning issues, there are also some attorneys who understand the concepts and who are doing a good job of protecting their clients and addressing their needs. But they are still not doing the best job they could. It's the extra care and thoroughness that can give people 100 percent of all possible protection versus the 70 percent of what the attorney feels are the most important protections. Here are two typical signs your attorney may be doing a good job but not the best job possible:

- They insist on drafting separate revocable trusts because of estate tax problems with having a joint trust.

- If your combined estates are greater than $5 million, then there is nothing else you can do to avoid estate taxes.

Here the attorneys are showing they understand estate tax implications, which is big step ahead of some other attorneys, and they may be able to do a decent job putting together a life and estate plan for you and your spouse. But it also indicates they don't have some of the advanced knowledge to give you all of the protection and tax credits the law allows. With the right documents and language, married couples can combine most of their assets in a single revocable living trust and still obtain maximum estate tax benefits through other means.

Of course, if you find an attorney who understands all of these issues, then this guide is simply here to help you work with them. Putting together your life and estate plan should not have to be a hit-or-miss proposition, and it all starts by working with the right attorney and other professionals.

More Highlights of the Revocable Living trust

Because of the volume of books on the market which review the benefits of using a revocable living trust rather than a will, we will only cover the main points here. This guide is more appropriately focused on applying all of the life and estate planning documents appropriately. For a more detailed description of the benefits of using a revocable living trust versus a will, I recommend reading *The Living Trust* by Henry W. Abts III. For purposes of this chapter, the following are the main advantages of using the right revocable living trust:

1) Most property can be combined into one trust for two so you are acting as one family unit under one trust; there is no need to "balance" property between the two people and two trusts.

2) Distributions upon death are all handled according to the terms of the trust, with all of the "what ifs" and contingencies in place.

3) All assets in the trust before death and those transferring into the trust automatically after death do not have to go through probate. Because the assets do not have to go through probate:

   a. settlement costs are lower

   b. settlement times are much quicker

   c. the settlement process is private.

4) The revocable living trust is much harder to contest than a last will and testament.

Acting as one family unit

In setting up your joint revocable living trust, the two of you are taking on three roles—trustors, trustees and beneficiaries. As trustors, you are the people establishing the trust. As trustees, you are both jointly empowered to utilize the trust assets for the benefit of the beneficiaries. As the beneficiaries, you are the people who enjoy the trust assets. Together you both are taking control over all of the assets in the trust, together you are both running the trust for your best interests, and together you are benefiting from the trust.

In terms of owning everything together, a joint revocable living trust also allows the surviving trustee to immediately take over complete control of all of the trust assets if one spouse dies or becomes incapacitated. This allows for little or no trouble in taking control of just about everything the couple owns on a moment's notice.

Distributions upon death

Taking into account the "estate" part of "life and estate planning," couples naturally want to provide for each other when one of them passes on, but what happens when the second person passes on? There may be children or not. There may be favorite nieces and nephews, friends or siblings. How is property divided?

All distribution wishes for both people should be included in the revocable living trust, listing all contingencies. Most couples chose one of four main plans and then make some subtle changes. The plans are:

1. When one person passes on, everything goes to the surviving person outright and when he or she passes on, everything goes to beneficiaries jointly determined by both people; often children.

2. When one person passes on, everything goes to the survivor outright and when he or she passes on, everything goes to the beneficiaries of the second person.

3. When one person passes on, everything is accessible to the survivor, and when he or she passes on, all of the first person's separate property and one half of joint property goes to their beneficiaries, and all of the second person's separate property and one half of joint property goes to his or her beneficiaries. (For this, a separate property agreement is necessary).

4. When one person passes on, everything goes to the survivor, and when he or she passes on, everything is split in half with one half going to one person's beneficiaries and the other half going to the other person's beneficiaries

Let's use some examples to help make it clearer. Benjamin and Margaret are married, and they don't have any children. In putting together their joint revocable living trust, they decide they want to provide for each other. They have some different ideas to consider regarding who would receive their property after the second of them passes on. Benjamin has a friend John, and Margaret has a friend Kelly they each want to provide for.

In the first situation above, Benjamin and Margaret agree they want everything to go to each other first, and then sixty percent (60 percent) will go to John and forty percent (40 percent) will go to Kelly. Regardless of how property is listed in the separate property agreement, they wish to do a 60-40 split among the two beneficiaries. This scenario is not that common except in situations where the spouses have children, and in those cases, it is usually an equal division among the children.

In the second scenario above, Benjamin and Margaret wish to have everything go to the surviving spouse should one of them pass on. After that, if Benjamin was the surviving spouse, then upon Benjamin's passing, all of the property would go to John. If Margaret was the surviving spouse, then upon Margaret's passing, all of the property would go to Kelly. Because spouses are usually planning together, they usually wish to jointly provide in some fashion for friends and family members together, so the "all or nothing" scenario is extremely rare.

In the third case above, Benjamin and Margaret have a separate property agreement with their trust and each has some separately accounted property and some joint property. Because Margaret's career has been much more lucrative than Benjamin's, Margaret has more assets than Benjamin. If Margaret passes on first, then all of her separate property and her one-half of the joint property will be accessible to Benjamin during his lifetime, but the assets will still be kept accounted for separately. When Benjamin passes on, all of Margaret's separately accounted property and her one-half of the joint property will go to Kelly. All of Benjamin's separately controlled property and the other half of the joint property will go to John.

In the forth instance above, Benjamin and Margaret are leaving everything to the surviving spouse when one of them passes on. Regardless of who passes on first, the survivor will be able to use everything, and then upon his passing, everything would be split evenly between Kelly and John.

These are merely four of the most popular distribution methods using only one alternate beneficiary for each spouse. Life is not always this simple, and there are many more contingencies for which to plan. What would happen to Kelly's inheritance if she passed on first? If it were to go to her children equally, what if one of them passed on? Would it go to her grandchildren? At what age?

A good life and estate planning attorney or advisor will press you for more and more contingencies until he or she gets into some fairly remote possibilities. If you are not throwing up your hands in frustration saying, "My God, if all of those people are dead then I just don't care anymore!" then they are not pressing you hard enough for these contingencies. Most of my clients get to the point where they don't have anyone else they wish to name, and then they are either fine with their "next of kin" getting their property, or they will leave it to a charity.

Age considerations

Another consideration in distributions is at what ages should the beneficiaries receive their inheritances? As we mentioned in the problems with simply naming young beneficiaries on accounts and life insurance, most people do not feel 18 is an appropriate age to handle a large inheritance. With the revocable living trust, you can pick ages for beneficiaries to get complete control over their inheritance.

The natural question is what are appropriate ages? I can only go by what my clients have told me over the years, but I am happy to share their wisdom with you. Most of my clients concur 30 is a good starting age, since it is about the time most people become serious about life. If they have gone through a four- year college (and done so in four years), they have had a few more years to settle into a job or graduate school. And if they have gotten involved in a nightclub scene, then they have probably gotten the going-to-the-club-five- nights-a-week syndrome out of their system. That may be a good age to consider giving them control over some or all of their inheritance.

The other age my clients usually come up with is 50. If the beneficiary has not gotten their act together by the time they are 50, they are probably not going to, so there is no sense in holding the inheritance back any longer.

For most of my clients, they chose one or more ages between 30 and 50 for their beneficiaries to receive their inheritance. A popular scenario is allowing them to have one-third at 30 and the rest at 35. Of course, you can choose any ages you want, and you can even choose different ages for different people.

As a final note on beneficiary ages, this does not mean the beneficiaries will not be able to have funds before they reach those ages. The ages you choose are ages when they must have absolute and complete control over the assets. Until that time, the people you have listed as trustees will be able to manage the assets and spend money on their behalf. The trustee will be left with the discretion to pay for tuition to a college or trade school, but the trustee can decline to pay for training to become a professional skateboarder. He or she can agree to pay the rent for a one-bedroom apartment with trust funds, but can decline to pay for a 10-bedroom mansion.

Benefits of avoiding probate

There are a few extraordinarily important benefits of the revocable living trust directly related to avoiding probate. Because assets in a revocable living trust avoid probate, there are lower settlement costs, shorter settlement times and private distributions.

This is also a good place to talk about exactly why trust assets avoid probate. There are many attorneys and advisors who will tell you revocable living trusts avoid probate, but rarely will they tell you how it works. Well here's the big secret:

- Probate is nothing more than an elaborate process that re-titles assets.

- Probate takes assets that remain in the name of a person even after they have died and then distributes them to the proper beneficiaries.

- If nothing remains titled in the name of a deceased person, then there is no need for probate.

- When assets are titled in the name of the trust rather than an individual, when that person passes on, there is nothing to probate.

That's it. It's really that simple. It's hard to believe that probate attorneys have turned it into a multi-billion dollar a year industry. Whenever assets are in a trust, they are technically in the name of the trust and not the deceased person. Because the trust assets are not in the name of the deceased person, there is no probate. Now that you know how assets in the revocable living trust avoid probate, we can briefly cover some the benefits of avoiding probate.

No probate means shorter settlement times. With the exception of shorter processes that some states allow for tiny estates, probate is a long, drawn out process. It is common for probate to take somewhere between nine months and two years to settle, and some estates drag on for considerably longer periods of time. For example, Elvis' probate started on December 20, 1977 when the will was admitted to the court, and it lasted through August 22, 1989 when the file was finally closed. While it is not likely your spouse would have to wait 12 years for your assets to be available, there is no need to take any chances.

Avoiding probate also means avoiding extensive costs for appraisals, attorney fees and related costs of filling out unnecessary paperwork. While studies have varied on the exact costs, and it is different from state to state and jurisdiction to jurisdiction, the broad range costs may be between 4 percent and 10 percent of the estate assets. That can add up to some significant costs, which are not at all necessary.

Here are some estate values and corresponding estimated costs:

Estate Value	Estimated Costs
$200,000	$8,000-$20,000
$500,000	$20,000-$50,000
$1,000,000	$40,000-$100,000
$2,000,000	$80,000-$200,000
$4,000,000	$160,000-$400,000

At the time of this writing, some of the most comprehensive joint life and estate plans can be created for around $5,000 or less, and chances are, if the costs are higher, it is because tax planning is involved. By the time both spouse's estates are settled through the probate process, the costs above make the cost of a trust much more financially desirable than using Wills and having probate. Just in terms of cost savings, the trust is a better bet for all couples and even individuals, and considering all of the other benefits, it is still a must for married couples. And for a couple, the trust avoids probate *twice*.

Avoiding probate also means the settlement of your estate is private. In many states, probate court is like any other court where the filings are public documents. This means anyone can come off the street, see what assets you had when you died, who they are going to, and what that address is. Aside from the usual concerns of marketers, identity thieves and con artists seeing what accounts you had and the fact your loved ones are receiving them, many people feel it is simply no one's business. They're right.

I was once speaking with a financial advisor who provides workshops on revocable living trusts, and she always goes to the courthouse the morning before her workshop and gets copies of inventories for an estate that went through probate. At the workshop, she starts listing all of the personal information for the deceased person, the accounts and account balances on the date of death, and the names, addresses and dates of birth of all of the beneficiaries. During one of these workshops a man in the back row started screaming he knew the deceased woman and the presenter had no right to invade the privacy of her family like this. Well, that was exactly the point. She had every right to get the information because probate documents are public records. If you want to keep information private, then it should not go through probate.

By far, these benefits in avoiding probate would be worth the cost and effort in establishing a revocable living trust. But there is even one more critical problem some people have that the revocable living trust can help solve.

Living trusts are more difficult to contest than wills

As mentioned earlier, it is statistically much more difficult to contest a revocable living trust than it is to contest a last will and testament. For some, there is at least one family member they are at least a little concerned would create trouble. In some cases, there is outright hostility from a member of at least one person's family, or possibly from a disinherited child. Avoiding these conflicts may be on the list of life and estate planning priorities, so this is one more big benefit a revocable living trust has over a will.

So why, exactly, is the revocable living trust harder to contest than a Will? One big reasons is attorney economics. In most states, if a beneficiary (or person cut out as a beneficiary) decides to contest a will, then attorneys who do that type of work are often eager to get involved because they are fairly certain they will be paid out of the estate. As long as the attorney has something to "hang their hat on" in the dispute, they can ethically and financially proceed with the will contest.

On the other hand, if a deceased person has the bulk of their assets in a revocable living trust and has passed on, someone who wants to challenge the trust does not go through the probate court but instead goes to the general "civil court" process where it is much, much less likely that attorney fees will be paid out of the trust unless there actually is something fishy going on.

Now here is the important thing from the attorney's point of view. They are not public servants paid by the government. They are in business to make money. And it is much more likely you will be able to find an attorney to contest a Will where they are likely to get paid by the court out of the probate assets rather than get an attorney to agree to sue to overturn a trust in civil court. What usually happens is the person who wants to contest a trust is asked for $10,000 or $15,000 to get started, and the client generally says, "No! You'll get paid out of the estate when I get my money."

The reality is that people who want to sue to get something they are not entitled to rarely want to put up their own money to get it. And this is just one economic reason why it is much harder to contest a trust than it is to contest a will.

Summary

The right revocable living trust can provide the means for couples to bring property together and manage it as one family unit, upon death distribute property to the people they chose, take full benefit of estate tax breaks, and provide age and other restrictions. Properly drafted, executed and funded revocable living trusts in the $5,000 or so range also can avoid all of the negatives of probate, including high costs, long settlement times, susceptibility to challenges and loss of privacy. By using the right revocable living trust as the base of their life and estate planning, people can achieve many of their planning goals with relatively minimal cost and aggravation.

Chapter Four:
Living Probate

The middle-aged woman stood in the middle the bank floor screaming at the manager, her face distorted with rage and tears flowing down her cheeks, but the words coming through clear. "He's my father, he's in a coma, and you damn well better give me access to his money NOW!"

The people standing in line to make deposits took a step back, and one young woman with a toddler turned and walked out the door, gently nudging her child ahead of her while looking back.. "Ma'am, I've told you we can't do that…"

"You stupid moron, give me his MONEY!" she screamed. "I have to pay his bills or he'll lose the house, and I can't do that without access to his accounts!" If she saw the security guard walk up behind her with his hand on his taser, she didn't give any indication.

"We've already called the police," the manager said, trying to remain calm. "I know you are in a difficult position, but we told you to hire an attorney to help you get access to his accounts. Please leave now."

"How am I supposed to hire an attorney, idiot!" she yelled, turning to walk out the door. "I don't have the $5,000 the attorneys keep asking for. All of his money is in the accounts I can't get to!"

Gail watched as the woman stormed out the door, trying unsuccessfully to slam the glass doors behind her. Gail then walked up to the bank manager. "Wow, are you OK?" she asked.

"I'll be fine," the manager said, rubbing his forehead. "I really feel bad for her, but I can't just open up a client's bank accounts to someone without the legal paperwork."

He straightened up, composing himself, and asked Gail, "What can I do for you?"

"Unfortunately, it looks like my mother is in the same kind of situation," Gail said. "But all of her accounts are owned by her living trust, and I'm her successor trustee. I was told you already have a copy of her trust on file and paperwork showing I'm the successor trustee, but here's the form from your bank that is signed by the doctors declaring her unable to handle her own financial affairs."

The manager took the form and looked it over, a slightly skeptical look coming over his face for a moment. But only a moment. "Here are the business cards of the doctors at the hospital," Gail said. "They said if there were any questions to call them."

"That's not necessary," the manager said. "I've worked with a few living trusts before, and it appears that everything is in order. Come with me, we'll pull up your father's file, and hopefully we can get you access to his accounts by this afternoon."

While most attorneys focus on the "estate" part of life and estate planning, there are huge potential problems with a person becoming gravely ill but not passing on. And, believe it or not, having the right documents in place is far simpler and inexpensive than planning for an estate, but the revocable living trust can greatly help in this situation. For about $5,000, it would have saved the exact amount the middle-aged woman was trying to find to hire an attorney to handle the competency proceedings. The right revocable living trust and accompanying documents can also help avoid *living probate*.

Living Probate is not a legal term, but instead it refers to incapacity and the complicated, costly, aggravating, and humiliating process of declaring a person incompetent and assigning them a legal guardian (sometimes called a conservator). Basically, when someone suffers an injury or debilitating disease that affects their ability to care for themselves, someone needs to step in and take care of them.

The question is how easy do you want this process to be for your loved ones if you are the person incapacitated? How expensive do you want it to be? How long do you want the process to take control? For most, the easier the better, the less expensive the better, and the quicker the better. There are several severe problems associated with living probate, including a period of time where finances are frozen, uncertainty of control, and the expenses of having finances and health care decisions turned over to other people. And there are documents to help in this area, but, unfortunately, there are still a lot of attorneys who look at these documents as a nuisance simply because they are inexpensive and avoid legal problems they could be paid for in the future.

The Revocable Living Trust

The Revocable Living Trust is a highly effective tool for avoiding problems, expenses and delays when someone passes on, but it is also a godsend if someone becomes incapacitated. A good trust will contain provisions dealing with incapacity, including the process for removing the person as a trustee, replacing them with another trustee, and then the conditions under which the person can take back their trusteeship when they recover. And from there, the trustee is the person handling all of the assets in the trust to take care of you.

No court proceedings. No frozen trust assets. No delays. It all happens according to the terms of the trust.

In the case of a joint trust, when one person becomes ill, the other trustee is there to simply take over. For spouses and partners alike, the other person typically does not need any procedures or formalities to start utilizing the trust assets. The only instances where some paperwork may be needed may be to stop the ill person from using their assets. There are plenty of people suffering from the beginning stages of Alzheimer's or dementia, but they may seem perfectly fine to a bank teller or financial firm. In order to take away their authority to handle accounts within a trust, it is typical (for good revocable living trusts) to have 2 physicians certify in writing that they can not handle these matters themselves.

Another situation may be if there is a single person in charge of a trust, or if it is a joint trust the other trustee has passed on or is incapacitated. In that case the physicians certainly have to declare the trustee unable to handle their own affairs, and then the terms of the trust name a "successor trustee" who can step in and begin handling things. In this case, once the trustee has been declared unable to handle things, the successor trustee can immediately start managing the assets during the time of illness.

Conversely, once the person has recovered, physicians can attest that the person can now handle things themselves and they can be reinstated as trustee. Far too often inferior trusts do not provide for the reinstatement of the person as a trustee, so it is conceivable that they may be cut off from controlling their trust. Of course, it is likely that the person can go to court to legally reclaim their trust, but that involves paying an attorney to handle that proceeding.

Let me be clear about this—in a correctly drafted, executed, and funded revocable living trust, the successor trustee can handle all assets controlled by the trust during a time of illness. If accounts have not been transferred into the name of the trust, then the trustee is not allowed to control them. For those assets, there is a durable general power of attorney.

The Durable General Power of Attorney

The durable general power of attorney can be an extremely useful document during a time of medical crisis. Second only to the revocable living trust in terms of importance, the power of attorney can help someone take control of an ill person's non-trust assets during incapacity.

As previously mentioned, there are some strong income tax benefits to keeping retirement accounts in an individual's name. During incapacity, a durable general power of attorney may become critical to reaching the money in those accounts to pay for medical or other expenses. Even with the best Revocable Living Trust in the world, retirement accounts outside of the control of the trust still need a power of attorney for access. Otherwise, the court proceedings are needed.

Another important factor in working with assets for an incapacitated person is making sure all of the assets that can be inside the trust do end up inside the trust. Far too often, revocable living trusts are left unfunded or there are a few accounts opened up after the trust is formed and they are titled in the person's individual name rather than the name of the trust. Therefore, an important provision in the power of attorney is the ability for the power of attorney agent to transfer assets into the name of the trust and complete the funding process.

One other important use for a durable general power of attorney is in case of stubbornness or an inability to grasp the concept of a trust. Many times the people handling changes to accounts or allowing access to accounts are not familiar with the concept of a revocable living trust. However, it is far more likely that these same people have been instructed on the use of a power of attorney. Therefore, having a power of attorney on hand can still assist with trust assets.

The Health Care Power of Attorney

One of the most common horror stories for married couples revolves around one spouse dying, the survivor falling ill, and multiple children with conflicting views bickering while the doctors and hospital wait for orders to help the dying parent. If the parent had a health care power of attorney, they could have assigned one child, or someone completely different, to make their medical decisions if they are not able to. The situation is worse for unmarried couples where family members may swoop in and take control of health care decisions, kicking out the partner and not even letting them see their loved one. Having a health care power of attorney allows the partners to assign each other as the primary health care agent and then each person can list their contingent agents.

One of the most important things to keep in mind with a health care power of attorney is that decisions between health care and finances can be kept completely separate. A health care agent can be different from a trustee and power of attorney, and this often helps people who are trying to find "the perfect person" to handle everything. There is no need. One person can be in charge of health care and another can be in charge of finances.

When it comes to health care items, there is a strict division of duties between the trustee/power of attorney and the health care agent. The health care agent is empowered to make all health and medical decisions. They are not required or allowed to handle the medical bills. That is up to the trustee/power of attorney. So the person you feel best able to make the best medical decisions can make those decisions, and the person you feel best able to handle finances can use your assets to pay for the medical care.

One thing that should be similar in the durable power of attorney, the revocable living trust, and the health care power of attorney documents is that they all should contain waiver language regarding the Health Insurance Portability and Accountability Act of 1996. This Act was well-intended and extremely effective in stopping doctors and health care providers from selling personal medical information to marketing companies. However, there are certain aspects of the law that make it difficult for someone else to make medical decisions for you. While it sounds nonsensical, your health care agent would be fully empowered to make medical decisions for you under a health care power of attorney, but the law would prevent doctors from giving you medical information in order to make a decision. The same goes for a durable general power of attorney. The power of attorney agent could be fully empowered to pay all medical bills, but hospitals would be legally barred from providing an itemized bill. HIPAA waiver language should be incorporated in both documents or as a separate waiver document.

It is also common for health care power of attorney documents to incorporate language regarding the agent making end of life decisions, such as keeping or withdrawing life support or artificial nutrition and hydration. However, most of my clients prefer to make those critical decisions themselves ahead of time in a Living Will. For more information on Living Wills (also known as Advance Health Care Directives), please read *Estate Planning for Married Couples* available at www.PlainEnglishAttorney.com.

Summary

While a Revocable Living Trust can be a crucial part of an integrated estate plan, it can also become an extremely important part of helping a family manage assets during a medical crisis. When used in conjunction with a health care power of attorney and durable general power of attorney, living probate and all of its accompanying costs, delays, and aggravation can be avoided.

Chapter Five:
Funding the Trust

We sat at the kitchen table reviewing their father's trust. Mr. John Smith (not his real name) had passed on a week earlier, finally succumbing to cancer. While his children had prepared themselves, Mr. Smith had prepared even more. He had one of the best trusts around, created by a California attorney two years earlier. "My father wanted to keep settling things as simple as possible," the daughter said. "That's why he basically liquidated everything and put it into a checking account in the name of the trust."

"That will really make things simple," I said. "As long as all of the medical and other bills are paid, there's no reason not to distribute the funds within the next few weeks. Are you sure that all he had was the one bank account and it was in the name of the trust?"

"Well, yeah," the daughter replied. "Except for these three stocks he wanted to hold on to. They're in his name, not the name of the trust… is that a problem?"

I tried not to sigh too visibly, realizing that while the trust could be settled in the next few weeks, it may be months or up to a year before the stocks were distributed through the probate process.

Once you have a revocable living trust in place, you have to make sure all of your assets work with your trust. In other words, you have to make sure your revocable living trust is funded properly. A revocable living trust will keep all of the assets in the trust from having to go through probate. Therefore, to avoid probate completely, you have to make sure all of your assets are in the trust or are set up to transfer into the trust upon death. Even with the best $5,000 revocable living trust money can buy, without funding it properly, all you really have is an expensive Will.

Here is where many attorneys put one over on their clients when they are approached about putting together a revocable living trust. Rather than advise their clients on the funding of the trust, they simply put together the documents and say, "OK, you're done. You have a revocable living trust." But then someone passes on, and the trust becomes nothing more than a receptacle for assets after they go through the probate process. And that is where revocable living trusts can get a bad reputation.

Most of the problems people hear about revocable living trusts are just like the stories people hear about hospitals. There is nothing inherently wrong with hospitals. Hospitals and the people who work in them can save your life, help you recover and then release you from their care allowing you to have a longer or better life. But then there are the stories of medication mix-ups, surgeries happening on the wrong person or the wrong part of the body, or a host of other malpractice problems. But all of these problems stem from the practice of medicine being done poorly.

It is the same with a revocable living trust not being effective in doing what it is supposed to do—avoid probate, preserve privacy, lower costs and shorten settlement times. The main area where revocable trusts fall short is when assets are not set up properly to work in conjunction with the trust. And so the revocable living trust naysayers, who are mostly attorneys who do a lot of probate work (big surprise), are way off target when they suggest people not use revocable trusts at all. What they should be saying is if you have a revocable living trust, just make sure it is drafted properly and your assets are in place to take full advantage of it. After all, no one is suggesting just because there are mistakes made in hospitals we should simply close them all down—we just need to make sure that things happen the way they are supposed to.

While each asset is a little different, there are three main kinds of changes that have to take place depending on the type of asset. If your revocable living trust was drafted properly and an "assignment of personal assets" or similar form has been used, then all of your personal assets like clothing, furniture and appliances are already in the trust. This even covers things like the food in the refrigerator and the change between the seat cushions. What we need to be concerned with are items such as real estate and timeshares, investment and retirement accounts, bank accounts and other assets that have some sort of title to them.

The first kind of change is re-titling an asset in the name of the revocable living trust. In short, you and your spouse/partner are changing these assets so technically you no longer own the asset but your joint trust does. But don't worry. You still control everything in the trust and can still do everything you normally would do as if it were property owned by both of you. The second kind of change is making the trust the primary beneficiary in case you pass on. You still remain the owner on the account, but now when you pass on it can go directly into the trust without having to go through probate to get there. The third change is to make a person the primary beneficiary and the trust becomes the contingent beneficiary. In this instance you keep control of the account, but if you pass it goes to another person, namely your spouse/partner, and not the trust. If the other person passes on before you do, then it would go to the trust to be distributed. *The most important thing is that all of these possible transfers happen without probate.*

While there may be different permutations and exceptions, these are the three main kinds of changes that need to be done. We will now go through some specifics on these changes one at a time, discuss which assets require a specific method, and then go into some exceptions, future steps and maintenance. But first, here are a few basics regardless of what kind of change is made.

The Basics

Always use the legal trust name and the legal names of people. The name of the trust is typically found in the first few pages of the revocable living trust. We also prepare a report for our clients called "Property Title and Beneficiary Changes & Designations" and list the proper name of the trust on the first page. This typically reads something like "The Revocable Living Trust of Jessica Tate and Mary Campbell." For a person's name, if their name is John Wilkes Booth or Lee Harvey Oswald, you should not refer to them as Wilkee Booth or Ossie Oswald, even though that is how people generally know them. Always use the full proper name.

One benefit of working with an attorney who works closely with financial advisors is that the advisor will typically outline and assist with a lot of these changes for clients using the exact names and information, and will also work with an attorney for any legal documents needed to make these changes, such as drafting deeds.

Second, always look at what kind of asset or account you are handling and ask "have I paid income taxes on this yet?" This is actually a big consideration. Any account that is "tax-qualified," meaning it is for retirement and you were able to put that money away without paying income taxes on it, should never be transferred directly into the name of the trust. If you do, then IRS regulations may treat that as if you had taken all of the money out in one year, and you are subject to taxes and possibly penalties. If you are in doubt, contact your attorney or tax professional before making any such change.

Finally, start with a list of all of your accounts and assets that have some kind of title to them and make sure you go through the list until all of the changes are completed.

Re-titling assets in the name of the trust

In some cases, re-titling an asset so it is in the name of the trust is the best course of action. This is certainly the case with real estate, and is best for mutual funds, savings accounts, checking accounts, money market accounts, and other non-qualified brokerage accounts. By non-qualified, I mean that you have paid income taxes on the money before you put it into the account. As a word of caution, unless you are working with an attorney who funds the trust as part of the process or works with a financial advisor who does, we encourage people to handle as many of the transfers on their own as they can to save on the costs of funding the trust. Our firm charges a few thousand dollars extra to handle all of the funding, but most clients can handle these items with the help of their financial advisor. However, transferring ownership of real estate and timeshares involves preparing a legal deed to make those transfers. Drafting a deed is something only a licensed attorney should do, so if this has not been taken care of by your attorney, contact him or her.

For more information, go to www.PlainEnglishAttorney.com

In making changes to accounts, the type of form you would need is probably titled something like a "change of ownership" or "change of title." In any event, your financial advisor or personnel at the institution should know which form is required to change the ownership of the account in the right way. If your advisor does not know, contact your attorney and have him or her speak with the financial institution.

Changing the primary beneficiary

There are also some situations where changing the ownership is not as beneficial as changing the beneficiary. The best example is a life insurance policy. The most important part of the life insurance contract is who gets the proceeds. In this case, the trust is the right beneficiary. While it is possible to make the revocable living trust the owner, the paperwork is usually much more involved and has no added benefit. Instead, it becomes easier to keep your life insurance policy in your name and simply make your trust the primary beneficiary. Upon death, all it would take is a copy of the death certificate for the proceeds to pay into your trust.

Please also note at this point we are talking about situations that don't involve estate tax problems. If you have large life insurance policies and may be subject to estate taxes, other steps can be taken to account for ownership of life insurance while saving estate taxes through an Irrevocable Life Insurance Trust, which is beyond the scope of this guide.

Changing the contingent beneficiary

Finally, there are a few situations where you want to keep ownership of an account, name another individual as the primary beneficiary, and then possibly list the trust as the contingent or secondary beneficiary. In all of these cases, you are naming a spouse or partner the primary beneficiary of an IRA, 401K or other tax-qualified account for income tax purposes, and then listing your living trust or named individuals as the contingent beneficiary. For married couples, there are special benefits regarding tax-qualified accounts in that the surviving spouse can do a "roll-over" when one spouse passes on, meaning placing the assets in the account into the spouse's own IRA and then take the money out when he or she chooses. In doing so, there can be some considerable tax-deferred growth, but the main catch is this is only available to spouses right now.

We also recommend this same set up be done for tax-qualified accounts for domestic partners even though they are not married. Our reason for making this recommendation is the funds are still going to the person they want, and if that person passes on first, it will still end up in the trust to be distributed to other beneficiaries when the second partner passes on. Under some recent federal laws, domestic partners have the opportunity to defer income taxes when they inherit their partner's retirement account. Also as a very recent change, if a same-sex couple gets married, then they have the same tax advantaged roll-over option as well. This is true even if they get married in a marriage equality state but live in a non-marriage equality state. (Be careful and consult your tax professional regarding any state level tax implications.)

Difficult items

And now, because we are not in a perfect world, there are a few items that present difficulties. First and foremost, there are automobiles. The main problem with handling automobiles, at least in North Carolina, is that auto insurance agents generally don't understand what we are doing in setting up a revocable living trust, and so they feel compelled to say your car is now a corporate vehicle, therefore the coverage is much higher and your premiums will go up. There is also no way to put a transfer upon death beneficiary designation on a car title, and therefore there is no way to have the automobiles avoid probate without creating hassles during life. But as I tell my clients, as long as your trustee has the car keys and the car is registered and insured, it really doesn't matter if it takes a few months for the car to go through probate.

The second item that creates some difficulties is CDs. And no, I don't mean the music kind. Certificates of Deposit are typically registered in the owner's name and can't be changed until the certificates become due without having substantial penalties. Therefore, the advice our firm typically gives is to wait until the CDs are due, and then if you wish to keep the proceeds invested in CDs, work with the bank to re-title them in the name of the trust at that time. Also, it may be worth checking with the bank to see if it can somehow place a beneficiary designation on the CD. Then it is probably easier to simply list the trust as the primary beneficiary.

Finally, while this is not really a difficult step in initially funding the trust, a lot of my clients have had some difficulty in refinancing a mortgage once the land is in the trust. This is not a legal difficulty or even a financial difficulty. The fact is despite the large increase in the use of revocable living trusts over the past 30 years and more, a lot of mortgage lenders still panic when they see the property is in a trust. *Don't let their panic affect you.* Typically all that is needed is a few pages of the trust faxed to the lender, or in some rare cases, a letter from the attorney. If your lender is still in a panic or requires you to transfer your property back into your name before it will refinance, then it may be time to consider another mortgage lender. If not, then one deed must be created and executed transferring the land back into your individual name, and then a second deed should be executed after the refinancing is completed in order to transfer the property back into the trust.

We have gone over all of the different kinds of transfers, the different kinds of assets, what needs to be done to each, and even reviewed some trouble areas. If everything is done properly, your revocable living trust should now be complete and well-funded. But what happens next? As you go forward in life, there will be many opportunities to open new accounts, buy and sell properties, and make transfers. Each time you have a new asset with a title or account name on it, something needs to be done to make sure it works with the trust. In these cases, simply review this program again to see what needs to be done.

As a word of caution again about mortgages, if you are buying property in the future and will have a mortgage on it, it may be more convenient, and certainly less stressful, to initially purchase the property in your own name, wait about two weeks, and then transfer the property into the name of the trust. In general, this just makes things run more smoothly.

With most situations in this guide, we recommend you consult with an attorney who fully understands life and estate planning. However, with regard to funding your trust, you may receive even better help with the financial advisor the attorney works with.

Summary

The right revocable living trust can provide many of benefits, but the trust only works if it is properly funded. In general, assets have to be retitled in the name of the trust, set up so the account pays into the trust upon death, or set up so the account pays out first to a spouse or partner and second to the trust or another set of named individuals.

Chapter Six:
A Complete Plan

"And this is what we call The Big Blue Binder," I said, laying the massive book on the table. "In here, we have all of the legal documents you need to achieve the goals we discussed, both during life and after you have gone."

As I opened up the binder, I watched as Karl and Sherry leaned in, interested in the contents. Like so many others, the middle-aged couple had been together for years and thought they were covered with a set of simple wills. Then they read my book The Anti-Probate Revolution, attended a seminar I presented for a community group, and were only now seeing that they could have so much more with the right legal documents.

"That's an awful lot of paper," Karl said, looking impressed and questioning at the same time. "Is this really going to cover everything?"

I started going through the different sections of the binder one by one, pointing out the purpose of each document as well as the extras included with the trust. In addition to all of the essential legal documents, there were sections for recording final wishes regarding funeral arrangements, organizing financial summaries, recording trust allocations, and archiving deeds, account summaries and life insurance policies.

"The binder can just be a place simply for storing your legal documents, or it can become an integral part of your life and financial planning," I explained. "Some of my clients use this book as the centerpiece in all of their dealings with their financial advisor, accountant, and attorney. They keep their financial account information here, copies of their most recent tax returns, their life insurance policies and property deeds. One couple even keeps a journal of their progress on New Year's resolutions each year."

For more information, go to www.PlainEnglishAttorney.com

As Karl and Sherry started flipping through the sample binder, they came across a section with fill-in-the-blanks regarding final instructions regarding memorial services. Suddenly, Sherry started to tear up. As an attorney working with clients on planning for the best and worst, I have come across many emotional clients. But this was the first time I had someone tear up at the sight of a checklist.

Karl, obviously understanding something I didn't, started hugging Sherry while looking towards me to explain. "Sherry was very close with her mother, and last year when she passed on Sherry was put in charge of all of the services," Karl said. "She arranged for a burial, church service, the music, everything."

"And it wasn't what she wanted at all," Sherry said, pulling out a tissue and wiping her eyes. "About three weeks after the service, we found a letter in her dresser giving specific instructions on everything she wanted to have done. Cremation, simple wake, specific songs for the funeral, everything."

Karl went on to explain that Sherry's mother and father had all of the "recommended" basic legal planning documents, "But there were a lot of holes to fill in, account statements to find, and other details Sherry had to figure out," she said.

Sherry finally recovered fully. "At least our children won't have to guess at our wishes," she said smiling, and began tapping the blue binder. "It will all be laid out <u>*right here.*</u>*"*

As with any machine, all of the parts need to work together and cover all a wide range of actions and contingencies. Putting the details down in one place for your loved ones to find can make dealing with the details of your passing a lot easier to handle… and give them more time to reflect on the good times with you. Here are the main documents needed for most complete legal plans:

- A Revocable Living Trust

- Financial and Health Care Powers of Attorney

- Living Will/Advance Directives

- Nomination of Conservator Documents

- Pour-Over Wills

- Nomination of Guardianship Forms

- Assignment of Personal Effects Form

A Revocable Living Trust

As the core of an effective legal plan, the Revocable Living Trust controls most assets, and it provides financial and legal empowerment to two spouses or partners, or individuals, over all assets. If a spouse or partner falls ill, the well person handles all financial matters dealing with assets in the trust. If one person passes on, the access to trust assets is immediate, and full inheritance is nearly immediate. Further, when the second person passes on, all of the contingent inheritance plans for both people are spelled out in detail.

To summarize the general benefits of revocable living trust planning compared to Wills, by avoiding probate administrative costs of between four and ten percent are saved, time delays of months or years are avoided, estate contests are stonewalled, and privacy is retained.

Financial and Health Care Powers of Attorney

While the Revocable Living Trust allows one person to handle most financial assets belonging to their sick spouse or partner, the Health Care Power of Attorney allows the other person to make all medical decisions during incapacity. Some of the most important decisions an ailing person wants their spouse or partner to make relate to medical rather than financial or legal, including decisions regarding medication, hiring and firing of doctors, and visitation during hospital stays. The Health Care Power of Attorney, while far simpler than the revocable living trust or Financial Power of Attorney, may become the most important document during a crisis.

For more information, go to www.PlainEnglishAttorney.com

Regarding financial and legal matters, the Revocable Living Trust is designed to handle all assets within the trust, but sometimes there are accounts and property held outside of the trust either by accident or by design. The type of account most often left outside of the trust is the retirement account. As explained previously, retirement accounts can not be retitled into the name and control of the trust without losing their tax-deferred status. In other words, if a retirement account is retitled in the name of a revocable living trust, then it is treated as if the entire account where withdrawn in one year with all of the income taxes and penalties due.

This is where a financial power of attorney can come in handy. By leaving the retirement accounts outside of the trust, listing someone as the primary beneficiary, and naming the trust or other individuals as the contingent beneficiaries, the account maintains its tax-deferred status. But what happens if money needs to be taken out when the person owning the account is incapacitated? The well individual can use the financial power of attorney to access those funds if needed. It is the combination of the partner acting as a trustee of the Revocable Living Trust and acting as power of attorney that allows a person to take control of all finances during a crisis.

Living Will/Advance Directives

The living will may be the simplest document in a legal plan, but it may turn out to be the most important one. Although the health care power of attorney allows someone to make medical decisions for you, the living will takes the final, most difficult decision out of their hands. When it comes to whether or not to administer life support and artificial nutrition and hydration at the end of life, a living will can express your wishes and directions.

Many people remember the Terri Schiavo case from Florida from 2005. In 1990, Terri Schiavo collapsed in her St. Petersburg apartment, and by the time she was rushed to the hospital had suffered severe oxygen deprivation. It soon became clear that she was in a persistent vegetative state, or extremely close to it.

Terri's body was alive, and she did not need to be on ventilators or other mechanical devices. However, she did need to be on feeding tubes and hydration. After several years, her husband finally decided to take her off the feeding tubes and let her pass on naturally. However, Terri's parents interceded and refused to let her go.

What followed was years upon years of court battles. Up and down the court system her case went, with multiple appeals, multiple rulings, and astronomical legal fees paid. Eventually, Congress interceded and took the case out of the Florida state court system and put it into the federal court system, taking a legal step never done before in what was always a state legal matter. Finally, fifteen years after she originally collapsed, Terri had her feeding tubes removed and she passed on.

Whatever your beliefs in this matter may be, the point is the same for all sides—if Terri had only had her wishes in writing, none of the legal battles would have had to take place. Having a living will handles this issue specifically.

Nomination of Conservator

Another important document to have as part of your legal plan is a document that nominates your conservator. A conservator is a court appointed guardian. In the event you are unable to handle your own matters, your power of attorney document *should* be all you need to make sure the people you choose handle your health care and other matters. However, it is still possible for a judge to stretch his or her authority and start a proceeding to assign you a conservator.

If that happens, it is critical you have a list of conservators in writing *you* prefer. If you have conservators listed, it becomes even harder for a judge to select someone else without a good reason. It is also good practice to make the people you nominated as health care power of attorney agents to be the same people nominated as conservators. The jobs are nearly identical, and the criteria for naming a health care agent are the same for choosing a conservator. This may be a "spare tire," but it is better to have it and not need it than to need it and not have it.

For more information, go to www.PlainEnglishAttorney.com

Pour-Over Will

All properly drafted and executed revocable living trusts take the place of the traditional Last Will and Testament, but there is still a need for a document called a Pour-Over Will. In relation to the other documents, its function is relatively minor. However, it can not be overlooked.

The only true function of a Pour-Over Will is to take assets that may end up in probate and hand them over to the trustee of the revocable living trust to be handled. If an asset is titled in the name of the trust, then it will not have to go through the probate process before being distributed to the chosen beneficiaries. If it is in the deceased person's name, then it must go through the probate process first. The only way to direct the probate assets to the trust is through the terms of the Pour-Over Will. As this is the guide designed for our clients to read before their Estate Strategy Session, if you state the password is "granny" then you will receive one hundred dollars off any trust plan.

While every effort should be made to make sure all possible assets are in the name of the trust or list the trust as a transfer upon death beneficiary of the trust, sometimes there are things that just can not avoid probate. For example, if a person files their income taxes but passes on before receiving a refund check, then the IRS will only issue a check in the name of that person's "estate," meaning it has to go through the probate court. Nothing short of timing a death correctly would avoid that problem, and so the Pour-Over Will may be a shadow of a traditional Last Will and Testament, it still may have its uses and should be part of any complete plan.

Nomination of Guardianship

While concepts of child custody and guardian ship could fill an entire book all by themselves, this is not that book. However, a legal plan would not be complete without at least having a nomination of guardianship form if you are the parent or guardian of a minor child or incompetent adult. By incompetent, I mean in the legal sense that they are not able to make many of the legal decisions adults can make.

For more information, go to www.PlainEnglishAttorney.com

Be sure to also take specific note of the name of the document as it is a "nomination" and not "appointment" of guardian. While laws and rules vary greatly from state to state, there is a general understanding that the guardianship of children and incompetent adults can not be given away like property. While the wishes of a parent or guardian go a long way in a judge making custody decisions after a person passes on, they are by no means conclusive.

When it is seen that many people go years upon years without revising their planning documents, a person who was perfectly suitable as a guardian five years before may have become addicted to drugs, been in and out of jail, or even moved halfway around the world. If a person passes on naming a friend or relative who fits that bill, then the need for a judge to make the final decision on who receives guardianship in the best interests of the child (or incompetent adult) is obvious.

While people would like for there to be an easy path to guaranteeing custody passing to the people they choose, there is no simple solution. But putting those wishes in writing *does* carry a lot of weight, and naming those potential guardians and backups, one at a time and in order, is a necessary part of a legal plan.

Assignment of Personal Effects

The revocable living trust is only effective if assets are inside the trust or set up to transfer into the trust when someone passes on. An Assignment of Personal Effects form transfers assets that do not have a specific title to them into the name of the trust. For example, furniture, appliances, clothing, and books are all personal effects that are transferred into the trust without changing a title document on each and every individual item.

This is not the case with items such as land and houses, bank accounts, and financial accounts. Those assets have to be retitled, the trust is named as a beneficiary on the account, or some combination of the two. Above all, simply having the documents is not enough. Your assets must work in combination with the trust and other documents to take care of you and your loved ones. Again, a good, complete, revocable living trust package will provide all of these documents and possibly more for around $5,000.

Summary

As you have read in this chapter, a legal plan may seem complicated and contain a lot of documents, but such a plan is merely complete. Handling the myriad of problems that people *may* face, whether or not such situations are *likely*, takes planning and foresight.

Now that you have the information necessary to arm yourself in creating a life and estate plan, it is time to take action. The probate attorneys have $25 billion a year riding on you and others ignoring this information. For your family's sake, don't oblige them.

98655797R00046

Made in the USA
Columbia, SC
03 July 2018